Inspiring
Women
Every Day

G000143920

September

PRAYER

REBECCA LOWE

October

THERE IS ALWAYS ENOUGH

ABBY KING

MIX
Paper from
responsible sources
FSC® C015900

WAVERLEY ABBEY
RESOURCES
OPERATING NAME OF **CWR**

Rebecca Lowe

Rebecca Lowe is a writer, speaker and media consultant. She graduated from Oxford with a degree in Theology, and then worked as a journalist. She has written for a wide range of organisations, including *Care for the Family*, and has worked as a volunteer press officer for *Tearfund*. She is married to Rob and has a twelve-year-old daughter, Stephanie.

Abby King

Abby is a writer, worship leader and primary school teacher currently making her home in Birmingham. She loves helping people to feel accepted, loved, encouraged and inspired.

Prayer

REBECCA LOWE

P rayer is one of the most important aspects of our Christian life. We pray together at church, in mid-week groups, in prayer groups, as well as alone. At times of difficulty, the prayers of others can uplift and support us. When we've done wrong, we can confess our sins before the Lord, knowing that He will forgive and accept us into His kingdom. At times of great joy, such as a marriage or the birth of a child or grandchild, we pour forth prayers of thanksgiving.

Not surprisingly, prayer also features heavily in the Bible. The word 'prayer' appears more than 350 times, and numerous individual prayers are also recorded. Jesus Himself prayed frequently and taught His disciples to do so through the Lord's Prayer (Matt. 6:9–13, Luke 11:2–4). He talks about prayer no less than 42 times and is recorded as personally praying 28 times.

Prayer is powerful! Jesus taught His disciples that the prayers of the faithful can move mountains (Matt. 21:21) and told them 'if you believe, you will receive whatever you ask for in prayer' (v22). What an incredible promise! When we pray, we are not just expressing our inmost desires, thoughts and fears. We are tuning into the vast, unquenchable power of the almighty, who not only hears but answers.

Over the next few weeks, I hope you'll join me in exploring more about prayer – how it can transform and renew us, as God's power breaks through into every area of our lives. My prayer for you is that you'll be uplifted, inspired and encouraged to bring more and more of your life under God's tender, loving guidance. May we learn to move mountains together!

Matthew 21:18–22

'If you believe, you will receive whatever you ask for in prayer.' (v22)

For prayer and reflection

Dear Lord, thank You for Your promise that when we pray, God listens. In our busy lives, may we find time to bring our need to You and listen for Your voice. Amen.

Quiet time

Luke 5:12–16

'But Jesus often withdrew to lonely places and prayed' (v16)

How often should we pray? I'm a busy mum, juggling a hectic schedule of the school run, after-school activities, work and home demands. If I'm honest, when I'm pairing socks or putting out the rubbish, prayer is usually the last thing on my mind! And yet it ought to be the first! The Bible tells us to 'pray continually' (1 Thess. 5:17). Prayer keeps us grounded in God's love and grace and ought to be the foundation for everything we do.

If we ever needed a role model for this, we need look no further than the life of Jesus. Despite a hectic schedule of public preaching, teaching and healing, there are numerous occasions in the Bible where Jesus withdrew from the crowds to pray. He began His ministry by spending time alone in the wilderness (Matt. 4:1–11). He prayed alone (Matt. 14:23), in public (John 11:41–42), before meals (Matt. 26:26), before making important decisions (Luke 6:12–13), before healing (Mark 7:34–35) and after healing (Luke 5:16). Jesus knew that spending time alone with His Father was an essential part of His spiritual life — and if it was true for Him, it's even more so for us!

We lead increasingly busy lives: did you know, we receive on average 63,000 words of new information a day?! But amid the hustle and bustle, let's make time and space to be still. The composer Debussy is quoted as saying, 'Music is the space between the notes.' Too much noise makes our notes clang and clash together discordantly. When we are stilled and quieted, our lives are more harmonious. Take time today to create breathing space between the notes and listen for God's still, small voice.

For prayer and reflection

Do you have a regular quiet time, perhaps in the morning, or last thing at night ? Try to make space this week for regular intervals to be still and listen to God.

*Cited in J.G. Koomey, *Turning Numbers into Knowledge: Mastering the Art of Problem Solving* (El Dorado Hills, CA: Analytics Press, 2001), p96

Lost for **words**?

Matthew 6:5–8

'Do not keep on babbling like pagans, for they think they will be heard because of their many words.'
(v7)

'll let you in on a secret: I used to dread open prayer meetings! A naturally shy person, I'd listen to other people's powerfully expressed prayers with a growing sense of unworthiness. What if I couldn't find the right words to say?

We live in a society which often values 'style' over substance. When we pray, it's tempting to think long, eloquent speeches are more likely to catch God's attention. But the most effective prayers are often very simple. Consider the shortest prayer in the Bible, in Matthew 14:30: 'Lord, save me!' Just three short words – but how much is conveyed in those words. Or the tax collector's prayer in Luke 18:13: 'God, have mercy on me, a sinner'.

Sometimes, we pray with no words at all. I remember once, at a particularly difficult time in my life, sitting alone in a church, the tears streaming down my face, feeling overwhelmed by God's comforting presence. That was a sort of prayer. Another time, walking through the park at the height of summer with flowers blossoming all around us, my beautiful Christian friend raised her hands to the sky and said, 'Thank You, God!' That was a prayer, too.

Prayer is simply a conversation with God. Sometimes we are filled to overflowing with eloquent words – and that's wonderful! At other times, a prayerful silence conveys everything we need to say. We may find written prayers, liturgies or hymns to be a useful starting point on which to focus our thoughts. What matters, ultimately, is not how we pray but the intention of our hearts. When we communicate honestly with God, He listens – no matter how small or simple the prayer.

For prayer and reflection

Dear Lord, I thank You that You are always listening and are always there for me. Even when I can't find the right words, I can always call on You. Amen.

Weekend

'Daddy will fix it'

Romans 8:35–39

'And I am convinced that nothing can ever separate us from God's love.' (v38, NLT)

When my daughter was three, she was given a balloon at a local funfair. We carried it carefully all the way home, but then disaster struck – the balloon popped. Smiling through her tears, she reassured me, 'Don't worry, Mummy. Daddy will fix it…'

Our human frailties mean that there are some things we just can't fix. Illness, bereavement, divorce, relationship breakdowns: all of these can leave a gaping hole in our lives that we simply can't mend.

How fortunate we are, then to have a Father in heaven who cares for us, listens to our prayers, and is able to restore us spiritually – from the inside out. He sent His only Son to repair the greatest 'gap' of all – restoring us from brokenness to a whole relationship with Him, through His death and resurrection.

No, we can't fix everything on our own, but we have a heavenly Father who is able to do more for us than we can ever comprehend or imagine. He is eternal, everlasting, and nothing, not even death, can separate us from His love.

'Daddy will fix it' – yes, indeed!

Optional further reading

J.D. Myers, *What is Prayer?: How to Pray to God the Way You Talk to a Friend*

C.S. Lewis, *How to Pray: Reflections and Essays*

WAVERLEY ABBEY COLLEGE

Higher Education Programmes 2021-22

Spiritual Formation Faculty

MA Spiritual Formation

PG Dip Spiritual Formation

PG Cert

- Chaplaincy
- Mentoring and Coaching
- Pastoral Care
- Spiritual Direction

BA (Hons) Top-up

EMCC
European Mentoring &
Coaching Council

QAA Reviewed
Quality Assurance Agency
for Higher Education

Counselling Faculty

MA Therapeutic Counselling and Psychotherapy

MA Counselling

BA (Hons) Counselling

Dip HE in Counselling

Leadership Faculty

MA in Public Leadership (distance learning programme)

This programme is subject to validation
Launching in January 2022

We also offer Continuing Professional Development short courses in Spiritual Formation and Counselling, including Counselling Supervision training.

To find out more call **01252 784731**

or visit **waverleyabbeycollege.ac.uk**

or email **admissions@waverleyabbeycollege.ac.uk**

Adoration: the wow factor

**1 Chronicles
29:11–12**

'Yours, LORD, is
the greatness and
the power and the
glory and the
majesty and the
splendour' (v11)

There are many different types of prayer. Some of the most common are adoration (praise), confession (saying sorry), thanksgiving (saying thank you), intercession (praying for others) and petition (asking God for something). This week I want to look at some examples, starting with adoration.

Have you ever had one of those wow moments, where you feel overwhelmed by God's presence and majesty? I had one such moment when I climbed Scafell Pike in the English Lake District, with a group of Christian friends. As we reached the summit, exhausted but triumphant, the mist suddenly descended, throwing us into a state of panic and confusion. Suddenly, we had no sense of direction – and no idea of how to find our way back down again! Just as suddenly, the mist lifted and we were treated to the most breathtaking, panoramic view of the lakes and mountainside stretching before us. As we clambered down, I was reminded of a phrase from the twelfth-century abbess, Hildegard of Bingen – we are 'feathers on the breath of God'.

In the mundanities of everyday life, it's easy to forget that sense of wonder. But today's passage is a reminder of the awesomeness of the God we serve. He is the God of the universe, heaven and earth, and yet He still cares for us! Everything we have belongs to God and every good thing comes from Him. When we praise God wholeheartedly, it eliminates self-pity, jealousy and pride, as we rediscover the truth of His blessing: 'Jesus Christ is the same yesterday and today and for ever' (Heb. 13:8). The Lord is worthy of our gratitude, praise and adoration. What a mighty Lord we serve!

**For prayer
and reflection**

**I thank You that in
the midst of my
confusion and
darkness, Lord,
You are there
waiting within the
clouds to shower
me with Your glory
and Your eternal
light. Amen.**

Confession: saying sorry

1 John 1:5–10

'If we confess our sins, he is faithful and just and will forgive us our sins' (v9)

M y daughter was three at the time. We'd been baking together, the oven was off and the cookies safely cooling on the plate. I left her for a few minutes while I went upstairs to the loo. When I came back moments later, she was sitting on the sofa, a cookie in each hand, with chocolate sauce all round her mouth, and her cheeks full.

'Have you been eating the cookies?' I asked. 'Nooooo,' she spluttered, through mouthfuls of crumbs...

When we do something wrong, it's only natural to try to cover our tracks and hope nobody will notice. However, God is not so easily fooled. He sees everything and knows our every move. If we try to hide our sins from Him, we're only deluding ourselves.

As believers, we're saved eternally and God desires that we would no longer sin. However, as much as we don't want to, we still can't help but slip up sometimes, owing to our sinful nature. St Paul sums this up very well: 'For I do not do the good I want to do, but the evil I do not want to do – this I keep on doing' (Rom. 7:19).

Because God is holy, our sin creates a barrier between us and Him (Isa. 59:2). However, God longs to forgive us! Instead of covering up our sins, we should confess them, believing that He will cleanse us from all unrighteousness (1 John 1:9).

God is the God of second chances – and third, fourth and fifth ones! In fact, when asked whether he should forgive someone seven times, Jesus replied, 'seventy-seven times' (Matt. 18:22). Just as a loving parent cannot stay angry with their child for long, so God longs to welcome us back into His loving embrace.

For prayer and reflection

I thank You, Lord, for Your wonderful forgiveness. I am sorry for all the things I have done wrong. I turn to You today, asking for a fresh start. Amen.

Thanksgiving: counting our blessings

1 Chronicles 16:7–37

'Give thanks to the LORD, for he is good; his love endures for ever.' (v34)

When was the last time you took stock of all the good things God's done in your life? In our busyness, it's easy to focus on all the things we've still to accomplish, yet fail to recognise the many blessings God has showered on us already!

Before I moved into my current house, I'd lived in a series of dingy, damp student flats. If you'd asked me what I wanted most then, I'd have said, 'stairs and a washing line!' Now I have those things, it's easy to take them for granted. Advertisers tap into our restlessness by offering glossy pictures of bigger and smarter homes, cars, luxury holidays and the latest technology, so that we're never satisfied with the things we have.

As Christians, we've so much to be thankful for! When we were still in a state of sin and death, God offered up His only Son to bear the penalty of our sin. Through Christ, we can freely approach His heavenly throne, confident in our eternal victory – praise God!

We have many personal and material blessings, too. I thank God for my husband and daughter, family, friends, for my home, for food, security, safety, and so much more.

Of course, there will be times when we don't particularly feel like thanking God, especially in times of adversity. God doesn't promise us lives free from suffering. But He does promise to walk alongside us, and we know that any trial we face today is only temporary. One day, we will be with Him in heaven, and all our worldly worries shall be a distant memory.

Whatever today brings, be it joy or difficulty, know that the Lord is with you, His love endures for ever and He will never leave your side.

For prayer and reflection

List some of the blessings in your life, such as salvation, family, friends, home, job, safety, financial security, clean water, food and drink. Give thanks for each one.

Intercession: for one another

A relative is ill in hospital. A friend has an exam coming up and asks you to 'send one up' for them. You switch on the news and feel overwhelmed by all the troubles of the world. When the problems we face seem too much for us to deal with, we can come to God in prayer. A prayer of intercession is simply a prayer that is lifted up on behalf of somebody else. It might be a friend, a work colleague, your local member of parliament, or even someone you've never met.

In the Bible there are many examples of intercessory prayer (cf. Gen. 18:23–33, Exod. 32:9–14). Jesus also prayed for His disciples (John 17:1–19) and for all believers (John 17:20–26) – including you and me! But you don't have to be a great religious leader to pray prayers of intercession. The way of prayer is open to all Christians, since we have Jesus as our great intercessor: 'Who then is the one who condemns? No one. Christ Jesus who died – more than that, who was raised to life – is at the right hand of God and is also interceding for us' (Rom. 8:34).

As Jesus has interceded for us, we too are called to pray for others. We are to pray for *all people* – good or bad, rich or poor, Christian and non–Christian. This includes our leaders and those in authority. There is nobody that is beyond God's grace, so nobody is unworthy of our prayers. In fact, Jesus commanded, 'Love your enemies and pray for those who persecute you' (Matt. 5:44). God calls all Christians to be intercessors – what a wonderful gift and a privilege, to be able to come before His throne with our prayers on behalf of others.

1 Timothy 2:1–8

'I urge, then… that petitions, prayers, intercession and thanksgiving be made for all people' (v1)

For prayer and reflection

Dear Lord, help me to be a bold intercessor. Help me to persist in my prayers on behalf of others, and reflect Your mercy and compassion. Amen.

Petition: saying please

Ephesians 6:18–20

'And pray in the Spirit on all occasions with all kinds of prayers and requests.' (v18)

Prayers of petition, asking for something, are perhaps the most familiar sort of prayers. But they can also be the most frustrating. In a multi-connected, hi-tech world, we're used to instant solutions. We press a button and cash comes out of a machine. We order a coffee and it's with us in minutes. But what happens when we ask and ask and still God doesn't seem to respond?

Paul, the writer of Ephesians, had certainly experienced that. During his time preaching the gospel, he encountered opposition, both internal and external. He was arrested, flogged, placed under house arrest, and even imprisoned – surely enough to make anyone give up! Yet, in spite of it all, his faith remained firm. How? He prayed 'at all times in the Spirit'. What does this mean? In churches, 'praying in the Spirit' often refers to ecstatic prayer, such as prophecy and praying in tongues. However, it doesn't mean just that (though it does include it). Praying in the Spirit means praying not just in our own strength but with God's help. 'We do not know what we ought to pray for, but the Spirit himself intercedes for us through wordless groans' (Rom. 8:26–27).

Also, Paul persevered. Throughout his turbulent ministry, Paul prayed fervently and in faith, trusting in God to answer, in His own perfect timing. With hindsight, we know that Paul's prayers were answered. Thanks to his witness, the gospel spread throughout the Jewish and Gentile population, and eventually throughout the whole world. If it hadn't been for the fervent prayer of a frightened man in prison, we might never have heard the gospel – imagine that!

For prayer and reflection

No matter how frustrated we might feel at not receiving an instant answer to prayer, we can be assured that God is listening and will answer. Persevere.

Weekend

Heart and soul

....

1 Corinthians 14:1–20
'I will pray with my spirit, but I will also pray with my understanding' (v15)

God asks us to bring our whole selves to prayer. Prayer is not just a meaningless ritual but comes from the heart. I love to sing! But the most beautiful singing in the world won't bring us any closer to God if it's sung with the wrong intention. God can see through our pretences. He despises our outward expressions of worship if they are made only to impress others (see Amos 5:21–27).

I love to use my mind, too. But being clever or well-read doesn't make you a Christian either. I love to worship. But going to church on a Sunday, praying, praising or speaking in tongues all mean nothing if we then carry on as though God didn't exist for the rest of the week.

A sincere Christian life demands our all. God doesn't ask us to leave our intellects at the altar but invites us to exercise our God-given intelligence and judgment. However, we're not called to have a dry, dusty faith – far from it! Prayer, praise and worship are a natural, overflowing expression of our joy and gratitude when we consider everything God has done for us.

Let's worship Him – heart, mind and soul!

....

Optional further reading
Sue Mayfield, *Exploring Prayer*

The **Lord's Prayer**

Matthew 6:5–14

'Our Father in heaven, hallowed be your name' (v9)

The Lord's Prayer (see also Luke 11:1–4) is the pattern or blueprint for prayer that Jesus gave His disciples. This week, I'd like to explore it, starting today with the phrase 'hallowed be your name'.

What's in a name? Quite a lot, as it happens! When I was pregnant, I remember spending many hours going through the 'baby names' book with my husband. Names were struck off the list for being too long, too formal or just not quite right. In some cases, names can give an indication of character. I have a beautiful African friend called Comfort and another called Blessing. In Welsh, the name Carys means 'grace', and Angharad means 'love'.

Names are powerful! There are several incidents in the Bible where people changed their names to signify a change of character: Abram, meaning 'exalted father', became Abraham, 'father of many nations' (Gen. 17:4–6); and Jacob became Israel, because he had struggled with God (Gen 32:28).

God's name is the most powerful of all. When we pray to Him we acknowledge Him as the Lord of all, God of heaven and earth. His name is hallowed. The word 'hallowed' comes from the Old English word for 'holy'. To be holy is to be set apart or honoured. By declaring God's holiness, we honour His greatness and majesty. It's hard not to say the word 'holy' without also thinking of the word 'whole', which sounds very similar.

This is the God we praise – the God of all wholeness, who heals and makes complete all brokenness and bitterness. The God who created the heavens and earth, yet still loves us, each one of us, as His children. This is the God we get to call Father!

For prayer and reflection

Thank You for being our heavenly Father. Hallowed be Your name. Amen.

Your **kingdom** come

Matthew 6:5–14

'Your kingdom come, your will be done, on earth as it is in heaven.' (v10)

When we see the word 'kingdom', we tend to think in terms of grand displays of royal power. Perhaps we envisage palaces, pageantry and parades. God's kingdom is not like this. It's a place where 'the last will be first, and the first will be last' (Matt. 20:16), where those who are meek, poor and humble are exalted whereas those who are (worldly) rich shall be sent away empty (Luke 1:53). It's a place where something enormous can grow out of tiny potential. Think of the parable of the mustard seed (Matt. 13:31–32), or the parable of the yeast (Luke 13:20–21).

To pray for the kingdom is to pray for God's will to be done on earth as perfectly as in heaven. What does this look like? In Luke 4:16–18 we get a taster: those who are poor are fed, captives are set free, sick people are healed. Matthew 25:40 tells us that as much as we do for the weakest in society, we do for Jesus. We are to be the working out of God's kingdom values in the world we live in. It is a prayer that all would come to know the conciliatory love of God, who forgives the sinner and brings healing, wholeness and hope.

God's kingdom is both a present reality and future hope. We look forward to a time when His kingdom shall be perfectly realised. Until then, we anticipate that coming kingdom by working out those kingdom values in our lives. When we pray 'Your kingdom come' we also pray that God will help us change our focus – from our own selfish needs, wants and desires, to wanting to live according to His kingdom values. Are you actively working to make His kingdom come, on earth?

For prayer and reflection

Lord, You have spread Your love to every corner of the earth. Help us to care for it. May Your kingdom come, and Your will be done, on earth as it is in heaven. Amen.

Our **daily** bread

'Give us today our daily bread.' (v11)

B read is a staple food; person can survive for a long time on just bread and water. When we share a meal, we often break bread together. In fact, the word 'companion' comes from *panis*, the Latin word for bread.

To the Jews, bread was a powerful symbol of God's provision. It played an important role in the Passover festival, where they ate unleavened bread, remembering the time of the Exodus, when the Israelites fled slavery in Egypt in great haste, taking only what provisions they could carry, and didn't even have time to wait for the bread to rise properly (Deut. 16:3). During their 40 years of wandering in the desert, God's people became hungry and bitterly complained that they might have been better off staying in Egypt where at least they had food to eat. In response, God rained down manna as 'bread from heaven', miraculously sustaining them (Exod. 16:4).

Jesus would have been well aware of this symbolism when he told His disciples: 'I am the bread of life. Whoever comes to me will never go hungry, and whoever believes in me will never be thirsty' (John 6:35). Jesus provides for both our physical and spiritual needs. Like bread, He is essential for our growth and wellbeing. Physical bread perishes, but His sustaining love is eternal.

For prayer and reflection

Dear Lord, thank You that whenever I feel like I'm in a spiritual desert You are there to sustain and nourish me. Amen.

When we pray 'give us today our daily bread' we remember that God is able to supply all our needs, both physical and spiritual. If we are in need, we can come to Him today, just as the Jews did during their time in the desert. If we are tired and weary, He will give us strength. He is our great provider.

Forgive us our debts

Matthew 6:5–14

'And forgive us our debts, as we also have forgiven our debtors' (v12)

We all make mistakes. Hands up if you have never done something you know to be wrong, had impure thoughts, or acted in a way that's contrary to God's will? St Paul sums it up: 'For I do not do the good I want to do, but the evil I do not want to do – this I keep on doing' (Rom. 7:19). We live in a fallen, broken, messy world, and we are fallen, broken people constantly in need of God's forgiveness and grace. It's a good job, then, that we have a merciful and loving Father. We can come to Him humbly every day in prayer, asking for the forgiveness He offers through the grace of His Son, Jesus Christ, who died and paid the price for our sins.

Just as we are offered forgiveness, so we ask God to help us forgive others. Doing this is difficult, especially when we've suffered personal hurt and pain, and when the person who hurt us shows no remorse. But we need to understand that forgiveness is as much for our own sake as for the person we are trying to forgive.

If you're finding it difficult, it may help to focus on how much God has forgiven you already. We were once far removed from God's love but have been saved from the penalty of our sin through the death and resurrection of His Son, Jesus Christ. Forgiveness is, first and foremost, about *love*. Once we accept the magnitude of Jesus' loving act for us, it becomes easier to extend that grace to others. When we do so, we may find that our unresolved feelings of pain, anger and bitterness no longer have such a strong hold over us. We can hand them over to God, knowing that He is a God of both justice and mercy.

'Lewis B. Smedes, *Forgive and Forget: Healing the Hurts We Don't Deserve* (San Francisco: HarperOne, 1996)

For prayer and reflection

'To forgive is to set a prisoner free and discover that the prisoner was you.' – Lewis B. Smedes'

Deliver us from **evil**

Matthew 6:5–14

'And lead us not into temptation, but deliver us from the evil one.' (v13)

' t's just petty cash... nobody will ever notice.' 'I know it isn't God's will, but He'll forgive me.' 'I know it's a lie, but it's only a little one...'

Are you familiar with the little whispering voice of temptation? I know I am! Often, what the world offers and what we really need are different things. We all have selfish wants and desires. We hate rules, and don't like being told what to do. Instead, we convince ourselves we can handle the consequences, and ignore the alarm bells ringing inside our head.

I grew up with pet goats. Unlike sheep, goats are very independent. Every so often, one of them would decide to leave the herd and go its own way. And inevitably we'd find them with their head stuck in a tree or with all four hoofs stuck firmly in the mud!

It's the same with us. We might think we're smarter than the rest of the herd; but the truth is, once we stop listening to the voice of the shepherd, we quickly get ourselves into difficulties.

When I look back over my life, there have been many times when a few moments of calm spiritual reflection would have saved me no end of bother. Praying daily against temptation is a useful practice. You could use the words of the psalmist David in Psalm 141:4: 'Do not let my heart be drawn to any evil thing or take part in works of wickedness with men who do iniquity'.

In prayer, we humbly admit our human weaknesses to God. When we do so, we stand not in our strength but in the strength of our Father and creator, who has already overcome every trial through the redemptive act of His Son, our Lord Jesus Christ.

For prayer and reflection

'Put on the full armour of God, so that you can take your stand against the devil's schemes.' (Eph. 6:11)

Power and glory

....

Revelation 4:8-11

'You are worthy, our Lord and God, to receive glory and honour and power, for you created all things' (v11)

Yours is the kingdom…
An earthly kingdom where the King comes riding on a donkey
A heavenly kingdom where the lowly are exalted and the mighty brought low
An eternal kingdom where nothing, not sin nor death, can separate us from the love of God

Yours is the power…
The power to forgive our trespasses and wipe the slate clean
The power to pay the debt of our sin so that we can be free
The power to restore and heal the brokenness of our world

Yours is the glory…
The glory of the almighty heavenly Father
The glory of the Son whom death could not hold down (Acts 2:24)
The glory of the Holy Spirit who dwells within us (1 Cor. 3:16)

For ever and ever, Amen

....

Optional further reading

R. Connell (ed.), *Our Father: Matthew 6. Famous Bible Passages*

The prayer of **Jabez**

**1 Chronicles
4:9–10**

'Jabez cried out to
the God of Israel,
"Oh, that you
would bless me
and enlarge my
territory!"' (v10)

This week I'd like to share some examples of powerful prayer in the Bible. Jabez is an obscure figure who appears in the middle of a list of genealogies. We don't know much about him, apart from this short, powerful prayer that he left behind.

Have you ever said of anyone, 'Oh, they're a right pain!'? If so, spare a thought for Jabez! He'd been named for the pain he gave his mother during childbirth – not the most promising start in life!

In ancient Jewish custom, names were symbolic and could also indicate your future. So perhaps his mother foresaw difficulties ahead. But Jabez defied the odds! He wasn't content to be labelled as a pain. Instead, he sought God's blessing.

We can learn from this. It's easy to let other people's negativity persuade us that we aren't capable of achieving much, but God knows better! He can see our true potential and longs to bless us with full, rich lives.

Next, Jabez asks God to 'enlarge his territory'. As a leader, Jabez wanted his spiritual territory to increase, to claim generations for the Lord of Israel. What about you? Are you actively praying for God to bring about His kingdom on earth?

Jabez continues, by praying, 'your hand be with me'. He recognised his dependence on God and His guidance.

Finally, Jabez prays, 'keep me from harm so that I will be free from pain'. Our sinful actions often cause hurt and pain for ourselves and others. Jabez asks God for His protection. God heard his prayer and granted him what he requested (v10). In fact, Jabez was counted as more honourable than his brothers. His pain had been turned to blessing!

For prayer
and reflection

Lord, when I face
pain and trials in
my life, I remember
that You are a God
of miracles. Help
me to trust in You,
just as Jabez did.
Amen.

Hannah's prayer for a child

1 Samuel 1:1–28

'I prayed for this child, and the LORD has granted me what I asked of him.' (v27)

Hannah was a woman who knew pain. She longed for a child but struggled to conceive. Living in a time when men were permitted to have two wives, her anguish was worsened by the cruelty of her husband's other wife, Peninnah.

Things reached a flashpoint when it was time to offer the annual sacrifice. Though her husband Elkanah generously offered Hannah a double portion, she still received far less than Peninnah – who received a portion for each of her many children, and taunted Hannah.

This is the context for Hannah's prayer. We're told she 'wept and would not eat' (v7). Her distress was so great that at first Eli, the priest, thought she must have been drinking (v14)! She describes herself as 'a woman who is deeply troubled' and tells Eli, 'I have been praying here out of my great anguish and grief' (v16).

What strong words! Often, we think of prayer as a reverent, even calming act, but here we have Hannah pouring her heart out to God. In fact, that's not unusual. Many prayers come from a place of deep anguish (cf. Psa. 22, 42, 60, 69). God wants to hear of the pain that's deep within our hearts, so that He can heal us and make us whole. We don't always have to put on a brave face and say, 'I'm fine'.

Hannah's prayer was answered. Her son Samuel grew to be a great prophet and she later bore three further sons and two daughters. God is abundant in His blessing! Hannah's wonderful prayer of triumph can be read 1 Samuel 2.

If you're struggling today, don't be afraid to pour out your feelings before God. He listens and longs to restore your brokenness, just as He did with Hannah.

For prayer and reflection

'Go in peace, and may the God of Israel grant your petition that you have asked of Him' (v17).

David's prayer for **help**

Psalm 3

'But you, LORD, are a shield around me, my glory, the One who lifts my head high.' (v3)

The writer Oscar Wilde once said, 'There's only one thing worse than being talked about, and that's not being talked about!' Perhaps for some people that's true, but being bad-mouthed by others can feel pretty miserable.

When things are going wrong in our lives, people might turn to us and say, 'Where's your God now?' and it can be hard to find an answer when we're already struggling. Our Lord Jesus Christ faced the same kind of taunt when He hung on the cross, with the crowd jeering, 'He saved others... but he can't save himself!' (Matt. 27:42).

If you're struggling with others who are testing your faith, this psalm, which is also a prayer, has an answer: God is your shield (v3). We're not that familiar with shields (except, perhaps, in fantasy films!) but God offers us protection. When we face opposition or struggle with difficult circumstances in our lives, He is like a protective fence, keeping us safe within.

David's psalm is defiant in its certainty. God is the one who lifts up our head (v3). He answers our cry. He is there is our sleeping and waking (v5) and with Him on our side there is no battle we can't win!

Even when others taunt us with cries of 'it can't be done!' we know that we have won already. We can be certain of this because we serve a victorious Lord. Jesus, who has already defeated sin and death on our behalf, now sits at the right hand of God and invites us to spend eternity with Him – praise God! Therefore, with David, we can say with confidence: 'I will not fear though tens of thousands assail me on every side' (v6).

For prayer and reflection

Lord, when I face battles in my life, help me to remember that You are my strength and shield. From You comes deliverance. Amen.

Expectation and Wonder

Advent with Waverley Abbey Trust

Spark up the countdown as we reinvent adventing.
Join us for events to raise your wonder and build your
expectation. Dare to believe again this year.

Discover events, inspiration, group resources and creative
spaces to help you reflect on advent.

 C2C Advent: Journey to Christmas

 C2C Advent: Unexpected Jesus

 Advent Together

Journeying together through advent

waverleyabbeyresources.org/advent-2021

Jonah's prayer for **rescue**

Jonah 2:2–9

'In my distress I called to the LORD, and he answered me.' (v2)

The story of Jonah starts with rebellion. Jonah was a prophet in Israel when God told him to go to Nineveh, the chief city of Assyria – Israel's deadliest enemy. When he got there, he was to preach against their wickedness and call them to repentance. But Jonah refused! He didn't want any mercy doled out to this hated enemy. So, thinking he knew best, he got on a ship and sailed in the opposite direction!

We're probably familiar with the rest of the story. At sea, Jonah's ship got into a storm. Believing it was God's punishment for Jonah's disobedience, the crew threw Jonah overboard. The next thing he knew, he was in the belly of a giant fish, where he stayed for three days and three nights. Now, I don't know about you, but I reckon I'd have given up hope at this point. But not Jonah! For that's when he prays his incredible prayer.

Jonah's prayer dramatically describes his emotional turmoil and terror. But somewhere in the middle, the prayer turns from despair to hope ¬ and suddenly something changes. Jonah, the rebel, realises his dependence on God: 'When my life was ebbing away, I remembered you, LORD, and my prayer rose to you, to your holy temple'.

God did not reject Jonah because he had disobeyed. In fact, He patiently kept pursuing him until he had a change of heart. That was good news for Jonah – and it's good news for us! Even when we turn away from God, He doesn't give up on us, but keeps on pursuing us until we have a change of heart. No matter how far away you feel from God, it is never too late to turn your life around.

For prayer and reflection

Lord, when I feel in a dark place in my life, help me to remember that You can turn my cries of distress into songs of praise – just as You did for Jonah. Amen.

Daniel's prayer for **mercy**

Daniel 9:1-19

> 'The Lord our God is merciful and forgiving, even though we have rebelled against him.' (v9)

Have you ever been on the receiving end of a fake apology? Perhaps someone said, 'I'm sorry you feel upset' without fully accepting the blame for hurting you? This is not one of those apologies! Daniel's prayer on behalf of Israel is a heartfelt, no-holds-barred admission of guilt, and an impassioned plea for God's forgiveness.

A righteous man, Daniel lived in turbulent times. During his lifetime, he'd seen his beloved nation uprooted, its leaders carried off into exile and its people made vassals to the foreign state of Babylon. Their beloved Temple lay in ruins. It must have felt like God had abandoned them. Yet Daniel refused to give up hope. He knew God wouldn't abandon His promise to free His people from their 70-year captivity and return them to their homeland. He longed to see this happen in his lifetime. Yet, at 80 years old, time was running out!

So comes this heartfelt plea. Often, when we pray for forgiveness we can act like naughty children, trying to hide our sin or shift the blame onto others. Daniel doesn't do this! Neither does he try to bargain with God. Instead, he appeals to God's mercy and grace.

Perhaps you find yourself in a position where you, too, feel you need to pray either for a person or a situation, or even for your nation. Often, it's easy to feel powerless and wonder if our prayers can make any difference. But the Bible tells us that 'the prayer of a righteous person is powerful and effective' (James 5:16). The prayers of one righteous person can change a life, a marriage, a community or an entire nation. Will you be that person?

For prayer and reflection

Dear Lord, please bless our nation and our world. Help me to know that You listen to our prayers. Amen.

'Not my will, but Yours'

....

Mark 14:32–36

'Everything is possible for you. Take this cup from me. Yet not what I will, but what you will.' (v36)

Gethsemane

There, in the darkness of the garden,
Words tumbled from trembling lips:
'Lord, if You are willing, take this cup from me,
Yet not my will, but Yours be done'.

And here, in this dark night of my soul,
While the world sleeps on,
I, too, pray, hoping against hope:
'Let Your will be done'.

Even though the darkness closes in
And the night feels victorious,
For I have glimpsed Your sunrise,
And it is Glorious.

....

Optional further reading

Bill Hybels, *Too Busy Not to Pray*
J.D. Myers, *What is Prayer? How to Pray to God the Way You Talk to a Friend*

How to move **mountains**

**Matthew
17:14–20**

'If you have faith as
small as a mustard
seed, you can say
to this mountain,
"Move"' (v20)

A mustard seed is one of the most insignificant of seeds – about the size of the head of a dressmaker's pin. Yet Jesus says that if we have even that tiny amount of faith, there's nothing we can't do.

There are times when God answers our prayers in a wonderful, dramatic way. Recently, a friend asked me to pray for her baby grandson. He was in hospital with an infection, his entire body swollen and turning blue. Some friends prayed with me and, within a day, he was sitting up in his hospital bed, smiling. Two days later he took his first steps – praise God!

But there are other times when we pray and nothing happens, and it feels as if God isn't listening. What's going on?

First of all, I want to dispel an important myth: you are not responsible for prayers being answered – God is. When we pray, we hand the matter over to God, asking for His will in the situation. I consider myself to be a woman of faith. Yet I'm also human and broken. There are times when my faith is not strong and it's all I can do to cry, 'I do believe; help me overcome my unbelief!' (Mark 9:24).

In difficult times, all we can really do is pray with as much faith as we can muster: 'Lord, Your will be done'. If you want to know what to pray for – pray for more faith! Because the wonderful thing about faith is that, just like the tiny mustard seed, it might start off small, but it doesn't stay that way. Where there is a tiny bit of faith, it can start to grow and multiply. And seeds are persistent. Seeds can burst their shoots through concrete and break up rocks. So don't give up! Where there is faith, there is a way.

**For prayer
and reflection**

**Dear Lord, please
help me to keep on
praying and
believing, knowing
that even the
tiniest amount of
faith can move
mountains! Amen.**

Pathway Into Prayer

Free download to inspire you to develop an enjoyable and effective prayer life.

Learn to persevere when prayers seem to go unanswered. With space for notes and personal reflection, you'll be prompted with ideas for how to pray.

Discover how prayer prepares the way for God to move. See how prayer changes situations. Learn what God promises to do in response to our prayers, and how to cultivate friendship with God.

To find out more about the Pathway Into Prayer, visit **waverleyabbeyresources.org/for-you-and-your-church/**

Steering wheel or spare tyre?

Hebrews 4:15–16

'Approach God's throne of grace with confidence, so that we may receive mercy and find grace' (v16)

Corrie ten Boom was a Dutch watchmaker who lived with her father and sister, Betsie. During the Second World War, they helped many Jews escape the Nazi Holocaust by hiding them in their home. Eventually they were caught, and Corrie and Betsie were arrested and imprisoned in Ravensbrück concentration camp. Her most famous book, *The Hiding Place*, is a biography that recounts the story of her family's efforts, and how she found hope in God while she was imprisoned. One of her standout quotes is this: 'Is prayer your steering wheel or your spare tyre?'

We can sometimes think of prayer as a last resort, rather like a spare tyre we lug around just in case we ever need it. When friends ask us for help, we say things like, 'I'm sorry, there's not much I can do, but I will pray'. But praying is 'doing something'! Prayer is powerful. As we read yesterday, prayer can move mountains!

The reason that we can approach God with confidence is because we do not serve a remote and distant Lord but one who has entered into our human sufferings. As today's reading reminds us, He knew what it was like to be tempted, so is able to empathise with us in our struggles. Yet unlike us, He did not sin, but became the perfect sacrifice, ascending into heaven to plead on our behalf. It is because of this that we can pray to God with confidence, knowing that He hears us.

Prayer is so much more than a spare tyre! It is a powerful steering wheel, driving us forward in times of difficulty, helping us to move over rough terrain and guiding us gently through the smooth. Let prayer be your steering wheel today.

For prayer and reflection

'The wonderful thing about prayer is that you leave a world of not being able to do something, and enter God's realm where everything is possible.''

' Corrie ten Boom, *I Stand at the Door and Knock: Meditations by the Author of The Hiding Place* (Grand Rapids, MI: Zondervan, 2008)

Out of the **storm**

Psalm 107: 23–32

'They cried out to the LORD in their trouble, and he… stilled the storm to a whisper' (vv28–29)

ave you ever experienced a storm at sea? I have! I was on a cross-channel ferry with a group of friends, on our way back from a spiritual retreat in Taizé, France. We were calmly eating breakfast in the canteen, when suddenly the ferry listed dramatically to one side. Within moments, the tranquil atmosphere had been changed to utter panic, with people running in all directions! We did pray – but not profound prayers. Our prayers were more of the 'Lord, help us!' variety. Thankfully, the storm soon calmed down, but it was a salutary lesson in how suddenly things can turn!

Not all storms are literal ones. Throughout my life, God has seen me through many stormy periods of broken relationships, financial uncertainties and personal setbacks. At times like these, long, complex prayers become irrelevant. Often it is all we can do to cling on by our fingernails and pray, 'Lord! Please help!'

The good news is that, when we do so, God listens, even when our prayers are not particularly erudite or profound. He knows our every need. In fact, Matthew 6:8 reminds us that He knows what we need even before we ask!

We do not serve a distant, remote God. When the storms of life threaten to overwhelm us, Jesus is right there in the boat with us, just as He was with His disciples on the Sea of Galilee (Mark 4:35–40), rebuking the wind and waves and telling them – and us – to 'Be still!' How comforting it is to know we have a Saviour who is not a dim and distant figure but right there alongside us, helping us to ride out the storm, and guiding us safely to clearer waters.

For prayer and reflection

Dear Lord, thank You that You are there to guide us through all the storms of life. Please help us to trust in You. Amen.

Keep praying

'Be alert and always keep on praying for all the Lord's people'.
(v18)

Over this past month, we've looked at many different sorts of prayers. We've seen examples of miraculous healing, heartfelt pleas on behalf of nations, prayers for deliverance and prayers against temptation. We've learned that prayer is essentially a conversation with God – and that it can move mountains!

I hope by now you've begun to realise what an incredible gift prayer is, and are encouraged to use it as often as possible. The Bible encourages us to 'pray continually' (1 Thess. 5:17). Impossible, right? Well, that depends on what you mean by praying. Of course, it's hardly practical to stop whatever you're doing and fall to your knees every ten seconds but, as we've seen, prayer is so much more than this. Prayer is an ongoing relationship with God. When we pray, we open a two-way channel of communication – we talk to God, and we listen.

Prayer should be like the background music of our lives, as natural as eating, walking or breathing. We can pray as we brush our teeth, walk to the shops or wait for the bus. We don't need to use long, elaborate or holy-sounding phrases; in fact, Jesus tells us not to (Matt. 6:7)! We can simply talk to God as we would to a trusted friend, and God will listen.

We can pray whether we're happy, sad, angry or anxious (cf. James 5:13). Philippians 4:6 tells us: 'Do not be anxious about anything, but in every situation, by prayer and petition, with thanksgiving, present your requests to God'.

What an amazing privilege, to be able to speak freely with our Lord, at all times and in all circumstances. Let's pray!

For prayer and reflection

Dear Lord, thanks for the amazing privilege of being able to pray to You. Let my life become a never-ending prayer to You. Amen.

There is always enough

ABBY KING

Luke 9:10–17

'Then he broke the loaves and gave them to the disciples to set before the crowd' (v16, ESV)

Everyone needs food to survive. When our stomach is empty, our whole body works together to send us signals that it's time to eat. Hunger causes our blood sugar levels to drop, causing irritability. Muscles in our stomach begin to contract, causing those rumbling sounds, and hormones are secreted to tell our brain that we need food.

In one sense, the story of Jesus feeding the five thousand is a down-to-earth miracle about meeting our most basic needs. The crowd is hungry, and Jesus provides them with food. That in itself would be enough to encourage us. But taking a fresh look at this familiar story can help us dig deeper into what else it might have to say.

Over the next month, we'll read the story several times, finding different emphases, and read other scriptures in the context of this miracle that appears in all four Gospels. We'll journey through four key verbs from the passage: 'taken' (or 'chosen'), 'blessed', 'broken' and 'given'. We'll consider how we have been chosen by God, who makes space for us and has compassion on us. Then we'll look at how we can hold on to gratitude in a world that so often draws us into a scarcity mentality. In our third section, we will discover that Jesus wants all of us, even the broken, leftover parts that we think aren't worth anything. Finally, we'll see how this story points us towards our connection with God, with each other and with the earth. We'll explore what it means to give and receive and serve like Jesus did.

Today, let's start by thanking God for the gift of food that feeds our bodies and spiritual food that feeds our souls, too.

For prayer and reflection

Thank You, God, that You know all our needs. Help us to nourish our bodies, hearts and minds with the good gifts You provide. Amen.

Become part of someone's testimony

Our Bible reading notes are read by hundreds of thousands of people around the world, and *Every Day with Jesus* and *Inspiring Women Every Day* have recently been made free in the UK. We want everyone, whatever their financial means, to have access to these resources that help them walk each day with our Saviour.

Here's what one Every Day with Jesus reader wrote to us:

Ever since I started using Everyday with Jesus, I reconnected to the Lord directly again. It deals with my day to day and minute to minute problems in details. Guiding me in the most solemn and right direction for a dedicated Christian living.

As we trust in God's provision, we know there are costs to providing this ministry. Do you have a passion for God's Word changing lives? Could supporting this vision be a way in which you serve?

A gift of just £2 a month from you will put daily Bible reading notes into the hands of at least one person who is hungry to know God and experience His presence every day.

Visit **waverleyabbeyresources.org/donate** to become part of someone's testimony, or use the form at the back of these notes.

Chosen

....

Isaiah 41:8–14

'I have chosen you and have not rejected you. So do not fear, for I am with you… I am your God' (vv9–10)

These verses from the book of Isaiah have been an anchor for me time and time again. Being chosen by God means we don't have to wait for something, or someone, to validate us. Our self-worth does not come from our relationships, our work or our appearance, but is rooted in our identity as God's beloved children. It can sometimes be hard to believe that, especially when people have rejected or abandoned us. But I often think about how Jesus chose the bread to feed that crowd of well over five thousand people. It was an ordinary, small amount of food that He could have easily despised, rejected or ignored. Instead, though, Jesus saw its value, exactly as it was.

I believe Jesus wants to remind you today that you don't have to be extraordinarily gifted, talented or successful to be chosen by Him. It doesn't matter to Him whether other people have chosen you or not. He sees you; He knows everything about you, and loves and chooses you exactly as you are. As you read these words, may you know again the delight, affection and deep security of being God's precious, wanted, beloved child.

....

Optional further reading
Henri J. Nouwen, *Life of the Beloved*

Chosen with **compassion**

Mark 6:30–37

'Jesus… had compassion on them, because they were like sheep without a shepherd.' (v34)

My friend Jean grew up on a farm and once owned a small flock of sheep. She said that when you want to take sheep anywhere, you have to go ahead of them. Goats need someone to drive them from behind, but sheep need someone to follow. Left to their own devices, they get into all sorts of trouble and are in danger of being harmed.

In our reading, we see that Jesus had compassion on the crowd because they had no one to follow or show them the way. Interestingly, in his Gospel, Matthew reports something similar happening with a different crowd: 'When [Jesus] saw the crowds, he had compassion on them, because they were harassed and helpless, like sheep without a shepherd' (Matt. 9:36). It's not a big stretch to imagine that our crowd were also harassed and helpless, with the added problem of being hungry. I'm guessing you can imagine times when you've felt harassed, helpless and hungry, too. But we can rest assured that Jesus is wholly compassionate towards us. He understands exactly what it's like to be a human being who gets tired and frustrated; who needs to eat and drink and rest; who needs love and care. Jesus is our good shepherd, showing us kindness and empathy as He leads us through the many twists and turns our lives will take.

As we listen for His voice, let's remember it's the voice of compassion. God is not criticising, controlling or chastising us. He gently guides us forward into what will bring life, wholeness, peace, justice and joy. He goes ahead of us, behind us and beside us, providing for and protecting us all the way.

For prayer and reflection

Take some time to meditate on and pray through the words of Psalm 23. Ask God to show you in a fresh way how He shepherds you with compassion and kindness.

Chosen and **welcomed**

**Matthew
14:15–21**

'"Bring them here
to me," he said.
And he told the
people to sit down
on the grass.'
(vv18–19)

A friend once asked me, 'How can I support you?' 'Feeding me really helps,' I replied. So for the next three years, she and her family made space for me at their dinner table at least once a week, sometimes more. I could show up after work in whatever state I was in, knowing there would be a warm welcome and a meal ready for me. Round that table, we laughed often, cried when we needed to, and prayed together too. That family welcomed me not only into their home but into their lives as well.

In today's reading, we see Jesus doing the same thing for the hungry crowd. Instead of sending them away, like the disciples suggested, Jesus invited the people to sit down. He made space for them, inviting them to taste and see His goodness, participate in His life and share in His abundance. Reflecting on this story helps us to understand that Jesus is extending the same invitation to us, too. As we saw yesterday, we are so often harassed, hungry and helpless. But Jesus doesn't send us away in those moments. He understands what we need and how we feel. He welcomes us just as we are, inviting us to sit down with Him, so we can participate in His life and taste His goodness.

In his book, *Being Disciples,* Rowan Williams puts it this way: 'We are seen, known and held, but above all we are welcomed.' Jesus will never turn us away, or tell us it's an inconvenient time. He loves and welcomes us exactly as we are, and He always will.

**For prayer
and reflection**

**Thank you, Jesus,
that You always
welcome me.
Thank You that You
accept me just as I
am. Please help
me to welcome You
into my life as You
welcome me into
Yours. Amen.**

'Rowan Williams, *Being Disciples* (London: SPCK, 2016) p33

Chosen and **enough**

''Here is a boy with five small barley loaves and two small fish' (v9)

I n this part of our story, Andrew notices a boy with a few loaves of bread and some fish. He tentatively mentions this to Jesus, while assuming, understandably, that it will not be enough to feed everyone. In essence, he's saying, 'here's what I have and it's not enough'. In my experience, it can often be a short journey from 'there's not enough' to '*I'm* not enough', a journey that many women are familiar with. We can feel it in lots of ways: we're not slim enough, not pretty enough, not clever or talented enough, not a good enough friend, mother, sister, wife, daughter. We notice what we have and who we are and assume that it isn't enough, that *we're* not enough.

As we saw previously, it would have been so easy for Jesus to label the boy's offering of bread and fish as 'not enough' too. After all, it was a tiny thing to give in the face of such a great need. But Jesus never does this. He doesn't despise the loaves and fish, rejecting them as too small to be of value. He doesn't ridicule Andrew and the boy. Instead, He accepts what they have to give. Throughout the New Testament, we find Jesus choosing to use the smallest of things – a mustard seed, a grain of wheat, a lost coin – to demonstrate that God's kingdom grows and flourishes from the tiniest, most insignificant of beginnings. When we're feeling like we're not enough, let's hold on to the truth that Jesus values and honours who we are and the gifts we bring, however small they seem to us. Let's remind ourselves that in His hands, the little that we have to give can flourish and grow, becoming enough to nourish others, too.

For prayer and reflection

Lord, please help me to see myself as You see me. Help me to accept myself as You accept me and to remember that You say that I am enough. Thank you. Amen.

Chosen to **belong**

1 Peter 2:4–9

'You also, like living stones, are being built into a spiritual house' (v5)

As we begin to understand more deeply that we are chosen and loved by God, it paves the way for us to experience the true belonging that we all crave so deeply. We were not made to live in isolation, but to be built together in community, like living stones, as our passage today points out. But truly belonging to each other can only come from being our authentic selves. As Christians, we often fall into the trap of believing that we should act, feel and think perfectly all the time. Shame over our mistakes and imperfections causes us to hide behind a mask of pretending we have everything together. As a consequence, we are unable to establish authentic connections with other people, always wondering if they'll reject or abandon us when they find out the truth.

I believe, however, that Jesus is calling us to come home to our true self. We do this by allowing God to speak the truth about us, by rooting our identity firmly in His loving kindness, and by learning to love and accept ourselves like God does. Only then can we show up in our homes, our communities, our churches and our workplaces as our authentic selves. Only then can we experience true belonging without fear of rejection. It doesn't mean rejection won't happen, or that it won't hurt when it does. But we will not be shaken because we know who we are and who we belong to.

When we live from this place of authenticity, we give other people permission to show up as their messy, beautiful selves too. We invite them to come home to themselves, to God and to a community where we can all truly belong.

For prayer and reflection

Father, help me to come home to myself by rooting my identity firmly in Your love. Help me live in such a way that invites others to find love and acceptance too. Amen.

Chosen by **design**

As we finish our week of reflecting on being chosen, Psalm 139 is secure place for us to anchor our hearts. In this psalm, we are reminded that God chose us even before we were born. He crafted us together in our mother's womb, designing each part of us with precision and care. He was there as our cells divided, our brain developed and our heart began to beat. He wove every strand of DNA together, formed every fingerprint, and watched over us as our fingers and toes wiggled for the first time. In response to this, the psalmist can only bow in worship, acknowledging that everything God has made is good. I wonder if we can recognise that we, as God's creation, are good too?

In a culture that worships perfection and outward appearance, it's easy to look in the mirror and notice all your flaws. The skin that wrinkles, the hips that carry extra pounds, the nose that is crooked or the hair that won't behave itself. Or maybe you look at your personality and decide you're too loud or too quiet, too sensitive or too headstrong? But in truth, God created you exactly as you are, and speaks these words over you today, and every day: *'very good'*.

Why not spend some time in Genesis 1 and Psalm 139 today and ask God to show you again all the ways that He has created you with purpose and intent? If it helps, write down those words, 'very good', on a card and stick them on your mirror. Each time you look in it, remind yourself that you are God's creation, chosen by design to be exactly who you are. You are loved, wanted, accepted and very, very good.

**Psalm 139;
Genesis 1:26–31**

'God saw all that he had made, and it was very good.'
(Gen. 1:31)

For prayer and reflection

Father, help me to see that everything You created is good, including me. Help me to understand that I am created by design and You call me very good.

Weekend

Blessed

....

Matthew 5:1–12

'Blessed are the poor in spirit, for theirs is the kingdom of heaven.'
(v3)

Our theme for the next week is 'blessed'. That's what Jesus did when He took the bread that the boy had offered – He blessed it. But what does being blessed mean? If we look at social media, blessing seems linked to things going well: we're blessed when we get a pay rise, a promotion, a good diagnosis or better car. But what about when things aren't going so well? Are we still blessed then?

Today's scripture helps us to understand how Jesus thinks about blessing. He tells us that we're blessed when we're grieving and when we long for righteousness. We're blessed when we're meek and merciful, when we're peacemakers and when we're persecuted. For me, Jesus' idea of blessing is summed up by the very first beatitude, 'Blessed are the poor in spirit'. In other words, we're blessed when we can recognise our own lack and our own deep need for Jesus. Let's keep in mind this week that Jesus blesses the ordinary, everyday stuff of life: bread, grief, mercy, suffering. We are blessed by knowing Him and by working with Father, Son and Spirit to bring peace, comfort and justice to our world.

....

Optional further reading
Liz Carter, *Catching Contentment: How to be Holy Satisfied*

The blessing of **Jesus**

The very first thing I want us to know about being blessed is that it is all rooted in this blessing Jesus receives from God the Father. The Bible tells us that our lives are 'now hidden with Christ in God' (Col. 3:3) and so His blessing becomes our blessing. We are co-heirs with Christ, so everything God gives to Jesus, He gives to us as well. His favour with God is our favour with God. His approval from God is our approval from God.

The beautiful thing about this story is that Jesus receives God's blessing before He does a single thing. There have been no miracles performed, no sermons preached, no tables turned over in the Temple, no death defeated on the cross, no resurrection Sunday. And yet God looks at Jesus and honours Him in front of everyone as His beloved Son. Jesus doesn't need to do anything to earn God's love and neither do we.

We are God's beloved children, with whom God is well pleased. When we've done something good, it's easy to believe that, but when we make mistakes or have a bad day, it can be harder to hold onto. But I believe that even on the tough days, we have to dare to believe that God's love is not based on our performance or the level of perfection we attain. God blesses us and loves us because we are His children, the work of His hands, precious in His sight; and because of who we are, and who He is, not what we have or haven't achieved.

Take a deep breath now and choose to rest your heart in the blessing of God. He says this over you today and every day: 'you are my beloved daughter, with you I am well pleased'.

Matthew 3:13–17

'This is my Son whom I love; with him I am well pleased.' (v17)

For prayer and reflection

Jesus, help me to hide my heart in You, and know in a deeper way that as the Father loves You, He also loves me. Amen.

Blessing of **hunger and thirst**

**Matthew 5:6;
Jeremiah
9:23–24**

'Blessed are those
who hunger and
thirst for
righteousness, for
they will be filled.'
(Matt. 5:6)

I n the Old Testament, justice and righteousness are frequently mentioned together. Having a right standing before God means pursuing and receiving His justice. However, they are not mentioned together once in the New Testament. That's because the Greek word for 'righteousness', *dikaiosune*, means righteousness *and* justice. So whenever we see the word 'righteousness' in the New Testament, we can understand it as shorthand for both righteousness and justice. Our key verse, then, might read: 'Blessed are those who hunger and thirst for *righteousness and justice*, for they will be filled' (emphasis mine).

It's interesting to notice that the blessing Jesus mentions here is found in the hunger and thirst. We don't have to be perfect before we receive this blessing, we only have to notice our desire – our longing – for what is not right to be made right. Doesn't that feel like a relief? As an imperfect human being who often makes mistakes, it's such a comfort to know that God blesses my desire to make things right, even when I stumble and fall. He blesses me in my ache and longing for what I don't already have and promises to stay with me in it.

I find myself hungry for righteousness and justice in many ways. I'm hungry for an end to war, starvation and disease. I'm hungry for an end to racism and inequality. I'm hungry to live in a world where we care for the environment and each other well. I'm hungry for every one of us to know we are deeply loved. Why not take a moment to reflect on what you're hungry for and ask God to meet you there?

**For prayer
and reflection**

**Father, help me to
know that You are
with me in all the
ways I hunger and
thirst for Your
righteousness and
justice, both in my
own life and the
world around me.
Amen.**

The blessing of **obedience**

I have to admit that I'm not very good at following rules. I like to make my own decisions about the best way to do things — an attitude that has served me well on some occasions and earned me a few speeding tickets on others! Perhaps you're like me, or perhaps you love rules because they help you to feel safe and to understand what's expected. Christians often like to think about the Bible as a set of instructions for how to live a good life, but the truth is that obedience to God is much more than simply following a set of rules and regulations.

Jesus summed up what it means to obey God in the verses we read in today's passage from Matthew 22. So how can we love God with everything we are and love our neighbour as ourselves? I would suggest that the two are more closely interlinked than we sometimes imagine. When we focus on loving God, delighting in His Word and growing in the fruit of the Spirit, we find that God's concerns become our concerns. We begin to notice those people on the margins whom God loves and longs to call to Himself. We recognise the ways that systemic injustice is affecting our BAME neighbours. We can see the ways in which poverty harms our children and stops them from fulfilling their potential. The list could go on and on. There are no rules for situations like this, except a call to love the people around us and be the hands and feet of Jesus to them. It is as simple and as complicated as that. Let's be people who listen closely for the Spirit's direction and be kind and loving to those around us. It's much more exciting than just following the rules!

Deuteronomy 28:1–12; Matthew 22:34–40

'All the Law and the Prophets hang on these two commandments' (Matt. 22:40)

For prayer and reflection

Ask God to show you who needs your love. Perhaps you could write a card, send a text or give a donation to make God's love a tangible reality for someone today.

Invest in your mental health and wellbeing

Learn online, at your own pace, and gain greater knowledge to better understand yourself and others.

Would you like to feel better equipped at supporting friends or family through difficult times? Perhaps you'd like some guidance to understand your own mental health or wellbeing challenges.

Whether you're going through a blip, or supporting somebody who is, these courses will help you understand how and why some people are affected in these areas. Through the Insight learning platform, you'll discover the value of a healthy mindset and ways to navigate challenges.

Insight into Anxiety

Anxiety affects many people today. Explore key issues with anxiety, and skills and strategies to manage and overcome it. This course offers insight for those who want to help others, as well as those who face issues with anxiety themselves.

Insight into Self-Esteem

This 4 session course will lead you through an exploration of the importance of self esteem and how as Christians it is rooted in our relationship with God.

To find out more about our Insight courses please visit

waverleyabbeyresources.org/insight

The blessing of **gratitude**

**1 Thessalonians
5:12–24**

'Rejoice always,
pray continually,
give thanks in all
circumstances; for
this is God's will
for you' (vv16–18)

**Why not begin
your own gratitude
practice? End each
day looking for
three things you
can thank God for.
See how it might
draw you closer to
Him, among other
benefits.**

Paying attention and gratitude go hand in hand. There's a natural progression from noticing the beauty around us to giving thanks to God for it. In her best-selling book, *One Thousand Gifts*, Ann Voskamp describes how a friend challenged her to find 1,000 things to be thankful for. So she set out to find three things she was grateful for every day, and the impact on her was profound. There is now a whole body of research to support the benefits of simply writing down those things for which we are thankful. They include better sleep, less illness and more happiness. Being grateful is good for us!

For people who follow Jesus, gratitude also leads us into a deeper relationship with Him. Gratitude reminds us that we are constantly in receipt of God's grace towards us. Everything we have is a gift – further evidence that God is kind and loving and provides for what we need. Giving thanks also helps us to remember our need for God. There are so many things we cannot control or do for ourselves. We can't control the weather so our food will grow. We can't provide oxygen for ourselves. We can't wash away our own sin. Expressing our gratitude to God helps us to stay humble as we recognise our dependence on Him.

It's important to notice that our Scripture reading does not say we are to give thanks *for* everything, but rather *in* everything. There are situations in my life that I don't feel thankful for, as I'm sure there are in yours. But I *am* thankful that I'm not left to face those things on my own, and that God can work even the hardest circumstances together for my good.

The blessing of **keeping watch**

A s He was about to go to the cross, Jesus asked His disciples to keep watch with Him, to stay awake and keep Him company in His most vulnerable hour. But they couldn't do it. They fell asleep instead. Of course, it is difficult to stay awake and attentive during the night, but it is also difficult to stay attentive to other kinds of darkness: sickness, loneliness, rejection, disappointment. As a society, we have become expert at numbing ourselves to all kinds of emotional and physical pain. But as followers of Jesus, we are called to stay awake and attentive to all the ways God might be working in the world, even in the midst of our own vulnerability and suffering.

When we begin to pay attention, it's not just pain we notice, but beauty, too. In today's reading from Luke's Gospel, Jesus invites His followers to notice and consider the birds of the air and the lilies of the field as evidence of God's work in the world. He's inviting us to pay attention to the beauty of creation, knowing it will reveal something more of God's story and nourish our souls. For me, this most often comes from being around trees. Something about them stills my spirit and settles my mind. They remind me that I'm part of a bigger story and that, whatever season I'm in, I'm still rooted and grounded firmly in the soil of God's love.

I want to encourage you to get outside today, if you can, or sit by an open window and just watch. Pay attention to any beauty you might see, and any emotions that might surface. Ask God what He wants to show you as you pay attention to Him and to the things He calls you to notice.

Luke 12:22–31; Mark 14:32–40

"'My soul is overwhelmed with sorrow to the point of death,' he said… 'Stay here and keep watch.'"
(Mark 14:34)

For prayer and reflection

God, who never slumbers or sleeps, thank You that You watch and wait with me in the dark. Help me to notice where You are at work in me and in Your world today. Amen.

Broken

....

John 6:12–14; Isaiah 42:1–9
'A bruised reed he will not break, and a smouldering wick he will not snuff out.' (Isa. 42:3)

I broke a water glass the other day. I knocked it onto the stone-tiled kitchen floor and it smashed into a million pieces. Some of them were big chunks, easy to spot and pick up. Others were tiny little shards, almost impossible to see. It took a good hour to clean it all up. Every time I thought I'd swept up the last piece, another one would glint in the light, catching my attention. When there's glass on the floor, you have to be thorough about picking it all up. Even the tiniest bit can cause great damage to anyone who might come across it with their bare feet.

As we consider our theme of brokenness this week, let's remember that God the Father always works patiently and thoroughly to heal us from every wound. He doesn't want to leave anything behind that might harm us or others. So we can acknowledge our places of pain and suffering in the safety of His loving presence, knowing that God deals gently with us. He meets us in the places we are broken and bruised, He doesn't cause more damage, but rather brings healing, wholeness, hope and restoration to all the places we need it.

....

Optional further reading

Tish Harrison Warren, *Prayer in the Night: For Those Who Watch or Weep or Wait*

Broken and **lamenting**

Psalm 88;
Isaiah 61

I t doesn't always feel like you're being a very 'good' Christian if you come and pour out your complaints before God. It might feel ungrateful, disrespectful or downright rude. But the book of Psalms helps us to see that all our emotions are welcomed by God, even the more uncomfortable ones such as anger, grief and disappointment. Psalm 88, in particular, lets us know that we don't have to put a brave face, or a positive spin, on things. We don't have to pretend things are OK when they're not. Sometimes we are suffering and brokenhearted, and it's not only healthy but necessary to cry out and express our pain in God's presence. In our long, dark seasons, sometimes that's all we can do. And facing the truth of our emotions and our situation actually turns out to be the path towards healing and redemption. After all, you can't find healing for something when you haven't even acknowledged that it hurts.

In our reading today, the prophet Isaiah paints us a beautiful picture of how the Lord will redeem our heartache. In the deepest places of our brokenness and sorrow, we are promised that Jesus will be there to comfort us, and to provide for us in our grief. Isn't it good to know we're not alone in all the mess and chaos this world sometimes holds for us? When we're honest with God, we give Him a chance to meet our needs and fill us with His comfort. We find that God's grace and care are still there, even in the most unexpected places, even on the darkest nights. And not even our loudest cries of anguish can drown out the whispers of His everlasting love.

'He has sent me to bind up the broken-hearted… to comfort all who mourn, and provide for those who grieve in Zion to bestow on them a crown of beauty instead of ashes' (Isa. 61:1–3)

For prayer and reflection

Thank You, Father, that You do not run from my suffering and pain. Instead, You hold me close and comfort me with Your love. Amen.

Broken and **gathered**

John 6:1–15

'He told his disciples, "Gather up the leftover fragments, that nothing may be lost."' (v12, ESV)

I've always been curious about the part of the story that our key verse mentions today. I wonder why Jesus would want the disciples to gather up all the leftover pieces of bread? Does He want to demonstrate the magnitude of the miracle He has just performed? Is He trying to prove that He provided more than enough food for everyone? Or is there a deeper truth He wants us to recognise here?

When I think about the broken pieces of bread, I can't help but compare them to the broken pieces of my own life. They are my scattered and fragmented thoughts. They are my weaknesses and failures, the painful things that have happened to me and the things I don't like about myself. They are the parts that cause me shame and the things I'd rather hide away. I don't want to own up to or acknowledge the painful or vulnerable parts of my own story. I'd rather discard them, leave them behind on the ground like leftover pieces of bread. But the Holy Spirit reaches out to those pieces with tenderness and care. He gathers them in, listening to the stories my wounds – and yours – tell, with patience and understanding. He brings healing and nurtures us back to wholeness in order that not a single part of us may be lost.

Our suffering may be terrible and terrifying. It may be deep and painful, but it is also holy ground. It is the place where we meet with God and discover His mercy and goodness. It is the holy ground where God redeems, rescues and restores us. It is the place where ashes are turned into beauty and we find that sorrow can hold hands with joy.

For prayer and reflection

Father God, gather up all my broken pieces and help me to know that You care about them all and deeply want to bring me to wholeness. Amen.

Broken for **you**

T he story of Jesus feeding the five thousand has always seemed to me to be a foreshadowing of the Lord's Supper; the public meal Jesus arranges for a crowd, anticipating the private meal He'll arrange for His closest friends later on. The symbols of the bread and wine serve as an image of the human experience: the wholeness and the tearing apart, the hunger and the provision, the healing and the wound. Wheat that once grew in the ground is crushed to feed us. Grapes that were once alive on the vine are trampled to quench our thirst. When we take the bread and wine, we remember that Jesus was broken in the same way: His body and soul were crushed and trampled as He bore the weight of our sin. Before anything else, the bread and wine remind us that Jesus loved us so much that He laid down His life in order that we might know forgiveness and acceptance as the Father's beloved children.

In communion, there is the invitation to remember that we belong to one another, to the whole family of God. We are each unique and yet we each come before God with the common need to be accepted, to be fed, to be welcomed, to be forgiven and to belong. The bread and wine symbolise both our diversity and our unity, and invite us to remember our connection to the earth that provided them, and that we have been given to care for and nurture.

As we eat the bread and drink the wine, we are renewing and strengthening our commitment to our relationship with God, with His people and with His world. Why not take a moment to meditate on each of those connections today and thank God for the provision of His son?

Isaiah 53:4–12; 1 Corinthians 11:23–26

'[Jesus] said, "This is my body, broken for you."' (1 Cor. 11:23, MSG)

For prayer and reflection

Thank you, Jesus, for these simple, yet profound symbols to remember You by. Help us remember that we belong to You and each other each time we eat and drink them. Amen.

Broken and **hungry**

**Deuteronomy
8:1–5;
Matthew 4:1–4;
John 6:25–40**

'Then Jesus declared, "I am the bread of life. Whoever comes to me will never go hungry"' (John 6:35)

For prayer and reflection

If you find a desire overwhelming you, try this simple practice of a breath prayer: take several deep breaths – as you inhale, say 'Jesus'; as you exhale, say 'You sustain me'.

Looking at today's Bible readings side by side helps us to see that hunger and being fed are themes that run throughout Scripture. The passage from Deuteronomy describes how the children of Israel wandered the desert, in their brokenness, for 40 years, all the while being fed with fresh manna, or bread, every morning. This was meant to point to a deeper reality: it is not just the bread that sustained them, but the word of the Lord.

Jesus reaffirms this in His own desert experience. After fasting for 40 days, He was understandably hungry. Yet He chose not to gratify His hunger on His own terms, but to remember that only God can give us what we truly need. For the Israelites, for Jesus, and for us, the issue is not that of being hungry. We are human beings with all kinds of appetites. Some are essential to our survival: food, water, shelter, clothing, love. Others feel like very powerful desires: sexual intimacy, respect, meaningful work, acceptance, belonging. All these needs and desires are good and given to us by God. But they can become all-consuming if we let them.

It's no coincidence that Jesus' declaration, "I am the bread of life" comes right after the feeding of the five thousand. John means for us to read it with that miracle fresh in our minds. Jesus is more than capable of providing for our physical and emotional needs. But He is also the Word of God, the one who is our ultimate satisfaction and sustainer. Like the Israelites, we are called to follow in His ways closely, because they lead us to the provision, joy, acceptance and intimacy we truly need and desire.

Broken for **new life**

John 20:1–18;
John 12:20–33

The beautiful thing about God's kingdom is that suffering and brokenness are never the end of the story. As Barbara Brown Taylor writes, 'new life starts in the dark. Whether it is a seed in the ground, a baby in the womb or Jesus in the tomb, it starts in the dark.' In our reading from John 12 today, Jesus uses the natural process of germination to help us understand something about God's kingdom. When a seed is buried in the ground, it continues to absorb moisture until eventually its outer casing cracks open and new growth can emerge. Jesus, here, was referring to His own death and resurrection. His broken body, buried in the tomb, was not the end of the story. He was raised to new life on the third day, and now offers that same life to everyone who believes in Him. All our brokenness, whether self-inflicted, caused by others, or just the result of living in a fallen world, can be the dark place that new life might begin. That is the great hope of the gospel. The Apostle Paul puts it this way: 'the wages of sin is death, but the gift of God is eternal life in Christ Jesus our Lord' (Rom. 6:23).

'Unless a grain of wheat falls to the ground and dies, it remains only a single seed.'
(John 12:24)

As you read again today about the death and resurrection of Jesus, I believe He wants to show you those shoots of new life that are beginning to spring up in your own life. Let's ask God to give us fresh perspective and renewed hope for all our dark and dead places. Let's ask Him to help us trust that, in the specific places of our own despair, God is redeeming all things and causing something new and beautiful to flourish and bloom.

For prayer and reflection

Thank You, Lord, that brokenness was not the end of Your story and is not the end of mine, either. Help me see where You are bringing new life out of my darkness. Amen.

'Barbara Brown Taylor, *Learning to Walk in the Dark* (Norwich: Canterbury Press, 2014)

Weekend

Given

....

1 Corinthians 1:26–31

'God chose the weak things of the world to shame the strong.' (v27)

Yesterday, we saw that God is able to bring something new out of our brokenness, just like Jesus did in the story of feeding the five thousand. It would have been a very strange miracle indeed, if the bread had been chosen, blessed and broken, but not given out to feed the hungry! In our final week together, we're going to turn our attention outwards, and meditate on our final verb: 'given'.

As we've been reminded, our brokenness does not disqualify us from giving to others. In the Japanese art of Kintsugi, ceramics that have been broken are not discarded, but rather carefully mended with lacquer, laced with silver or gold. The pieces that have been broken are considered more valuable than they were before, their cracks and fractures an invaluable part of their story. It's a beautiful picture of what Jesus models for us in His life, death and resurrection, and the life He now calls us to live in Him. As we consider the different ways that God might want us to give, let's keep in mind that being chosen, blessed *and* broken are all valuable, precious parts of who we are.

....

Optional further reading

Philippians 2:1–11

Next Issue

November

SPIRITUAL HEALTH M.O.T.

SALLY NASH

December

EXPECTATION AND WONDER

ROS DERGES

Available in a variety of formats

In **November**, Sally Nash will explore the topic of Spiritual Health, looking at four areas of spiritual wellbeing which contribute to our spiritual health: our relationship with ourselves, with others, with God and with the environment.

In **December**, Ros Derges explores expectation and wonder, unpacking God's story and how we are a part of it. Reflecting on the joy of God's intervention in human history, she'll walk you through devotions to prepare you for Christmas.

Obtain your copy from waverleyabbeyresources.org or from Christian bookshops.

Given for the **kingdom**

Luke 13:18–21

'The kingdom of God… is like a mustard seed, which a man took and planted in his garden.' (vv18–19)

You'd be forgiven for thinking that to give your life to God's kingdom, some enormous sacrifice must be required. We read about missionaries who were martyred, and people who lead huge ministries or give massive amounts of money to churches. It's easy to look at these people and feel intimidated. 'What can I possibly give to God's kingdom that will make a difference?' we asked ourselves, and assume we've failed before we've even started. But in these scriptures, Jesus teaches us that God's kingdom grows just as much through the small and unseen gifts that we give. Our repeated acts of generosity and kindness, faithfulness and service can be the mustard seeds that grow into a mighty tree offering shelter to many, or the yeast that works through dough to feed the hungry. I would like to suggest that, in fact, *we* ourselves are the gift that God gives. As Mother Teresa was famous for pointing out, it is doing small things with great love that makes a big difference for people. I may not have been called to minister to lepers on the streets of Calcutta, but I can serve the people that God has put around me with love, humility and kindness.

I want us to end our time together today by thinking about how we might extend God's kingdom in small ways right where we are. Perhaps you might cook a meal, make a phone call, send an encouraging text, listen patiently to a child, give some practical help or offer to pray for someone? When we give and serve with a good attitude and a heart motivated by love, we are bringing God's rule and reign of righteousness, peace and joy to the world around us.

For prayer and reflection

Father God, help me to notice small ways that I might care for and serve others today, with great love, that Your kingdom might come on earth as it is in heaven. Amen.

Given for the **marginalised**

Matthew 25:31–40

Father Greg Boyle is a Jesuit priest who has worked with gang members in Los Angeles, USA, for over forty years. In his best-selling book, *Tattoos on the Heart*, Father Greg describes the work of Homeboy Industries, founded to rehabilitate former gang members as they seek new lives away from the violence and chaos of the gangs. What stands out is Father Greg's approach, which he terms 'radical kinship'. It's the idea that in serving people, there is no 'us and them' only 'us'. It's not about what I can give to someone else, but about who we can become together.

This seems to be the heart of what Jesus is talking about here in Matthew's Gospel. Jesus so identifies with those on the margins of society – the poor, the hungry, the sick, the stranger, the prisoner – that He says whatever we do for those people, we're doing for Him. I think about some of the people who are on the margins in today's society: prisoners, refugees, children in care homes, those with disabilities or chronic illnesses. I wonder what it would look like to be 'one body' with those people – to feel their needs as my own, to meet their needs as I would my own, to love them as I want to be loved myself. 'Radical kinship' is a good term for this because it requires a radically different way of thinking about and acting towards others. Jesus gave very practical help to others. He healed them and fed them and spoke words of comfort and wisdom. But He never did it from a sense of superiority. He gave Himself to people in friendship and love, with gentleness and humility and we are His disciples when we do the same.

'For I was hungry and you gave me something to eat, I was thirsty and you gave me something to drink' (v35)

For prayer and reflection

Lord, thank You for the 'radical kinship' You have shown to me. Help me to show that same kind of love to others, especially those who have been marginalised. Amen.

Given for **generosity**

Luke 12:13–34

'Sell your possessions and give to the poor.' (v33)

We live in a culture that assigns value to people according to their economic contribution. Those who earn lots of money are deemed to be useful, successful members of society. Those who don't, or who can't contribute to the economy are stereotyped as lazy or useless, and devalued and dehumanised as a result. In this passage, Jesus teaches us a different way. He starts by addressing an argument about the unjust distribution of wealth between two brothers and tells us to be on our guard against all kinds of greed, because life is not found in the amount of money or possessions we own. He then goes on to remind us that our heavenly Father knows about everything we need and that, as we seek after God's kingdom, our needs will be met. We don't need to worry, or assign people to the categories of 'haves' and 'have nots' or 'deserving' and 'undeserving'. In God's kingdom, there is enough for everyone, and everyone is of equal value before Him.

Jesus ends this teaching with a call to generosity, which is the best way to guard against greed. Often, we think of generosity being to do with giving money, and that is certainly an important part of it. But I have recently been challenged to be generous in other ways, too. I've been challenged to think less judgmentally about people who are different from me. I've been challenged to speak more kindly to people I feel irritated by. I've been challenged to give my time by listening to people in order to understand them better. When we are generous in all kinds of ways, we are sowing the seeds of the kingdom and loving people the way God does.

For prayer and reflection

God, I remember before You those whom society sees as less valuable. Help me to extend generosity in my thoughts, words and actions for the sake of Your kingdom. Amen.

Given for **justice**

Isaiah 9:1–7;
Micah 6:6–8

Previously in our study, we've seen the close relationship between righteousness, or right living, and justice. The prophets Isaiah and Micah also make it plain that God's rule and reign is characterised by justice and mercy. But justice and mercy can often feel a far cry from what so many people experience. We read stories every day of poor housing, domestic violence, ill treatment of refugees, war, poverty, starvation, child abuse, systemic racial injustices. It can be overwhelming to consider the weight of the world's oppression. Our small acts of justice and mercy can seem like the tiniest drops in a vast ocean of human suffering.

'What does the LORD require of you? To act justly and to love mercy and to walk humbly with your God.' (Micah 6:8)

Today's passage from Isaiah brings me great hope, however. God has promised that there will be no end to the increase of His government and His peace. He is faithful to His promises and we can trust that His kingdom – His righteousness, peace and joy – will keep growing and expanding into all the areas where it is so desperately needed. And our key verse from Micah helps us to understand our part in bringing in God's kingdom: we are to act justly, to love mercy and to walk humbly with God. These sound like simple instructions, but they are not always easy to follow. Sometimes it will require that we examine our own bias or complicity with systems that are unjust. Sometimes it will require that we have uncomfortable conversations as we stand up for what is right. And sometimes we'll have to forgive people we believe don't deserve this. But as we walk humbly with God, He will give us all we need to bring justice and mercy to our hurting and broken world.

For prayer and reflection

Bring before God some injustices that you feel strongly about. Ask Him to show you how you might act in ways that will bring justice and mercy to those situations.

Given to the **earth**

Genesis 1:27–30;
Romans 8:18–25

'Creation itself will
be liberated from
its bondage to
decay' (Rom. 8:21)

The suffering of humanity and the suffering of the earth are intimately intertwined. In her book, *The Very Good Gospel*, Lisa Sharon Harper describes how the colonial era led to mass deforestation and soil erosion in Haiti, making it very difficult for people to farm there. So Haitians have become dependent on food imports from other countries. However, when global markets lead to price hikes, the people cannot afford to buy food, leading them to search through rubbish dumps and eat dirt mixed with sugar to satisfy their hunger. That's just one example of how the earth and it's people are suffering. We know that climate change, plastic in the oceans and toxic chemicals in the atmosphere are having a devastating effect, too. Creation is groaning and we're groaning with it. But that is not the end of the story. If we will humble ourselves to act and pray, then God promises to liberate our land from its suffering.

There are many ways we can respond and care for our earth. We can commit ourselves to living more simply, rather than contributing to the overproduction and overconsumption that is destroying the earth. We can take steps to minimise our waste through recycling and reusing. We can help to advocate for policies and practices that seek to curb climate change and protect the environment. God's original design was that humans would care for the earth and the earth would provide for humanity in a reciprocal relationship. Restoring that relationship is part of God's plan for redeeming the whole world, and it is our privilege and responsibility to participate in that work.

**For prayer
and reflection**

**Thank You, Father,
for Your beautiful
gift of creation.
Help me to see
where I need to
change and what
actions I can take
to help care for
Your world. Amen.**

Chosen, blessed, broken, given

Luke 9:10–17

'Then he broke the loaves and gave them to the disciples to set before the crowd.' (v16, ESV)

As our time together draws to a close, we come back to where we began, with the story of Jesus generously feeding a crowd of well over five thousand people. I'd like to offer you this blessing as an encouragement for you to take with you as we go.

May you know that you have been chosen by God, who loves you with an everlasting love. May you know that you belong to Him and that you are enough, just as you are.

May you know what it means to be blessed by God and to receive the blessing of Jesus. May you come to understand the blessings of obedience and gratitude, and may you know the blessing of finding beauty in the midst of your own suffering.

May you feel held in your brokenness and know the deep compassion and care of God who will never leave you to suffer alone. May you know that your brokenness is a beautiful part of who you are.

And may you trust yourself into the hands of God, to be given to a hurting world, that God's kingdom might come on earth as it is in heaven. Amen.

Optional further reading

Psalm 103

Notes

et Your **FREE** Daily Bible Reading Notes TODAY! (UK ONLY)

our favourite Bible reading notes are now FREE. God has called us back to e original vision of CWR to provide these notes to everyone who needs them, egardless of their circumstance or ability to pay. It is our desire to see these daily ible reading notes used more widely, to see Christians grow in their relationship vith Jesus on a daily basis and to see Him reflected in their everyday living. Clearly here are costs to provide this ministry and we are trusting in God's provision.

Could you be part of this vision? Do you have the desire to see lives transformed hrough a relationship with Jesus? **A small donation from you of just £2 a month, by direct debit, will make such a difference** Giving hope to someone in desperate need whilst you too grow deeper in your own relationship with Jesus.

4 Easy Ways To Order

. Visit our online store at **waverleyabbeyresources.org/store**

2. Send this form together with your payment to: **Waverley Abbey Trust, Waverley Abbey House, Waverley Lane, Farnham, Surrey GU9 8EP**

3. Phone in your credit card order: **01252 784700** (Mon–Fri, 9.30am – 4.30pm)

4. Visit a Christian bookshop

or a list of our National Distributors, who supply countries outside the UK, visit waverleyabbeyresources.org/distributors

Your Details (required for orders and donations)

Full Name: **ID No.** (if known):

Home Address:

                                                                  Postcode:

Telephone No. (for queries):   **Email:**

Publications

TITLE	QTY	PRICE	TOTAL
TOTAL PUBLICATIONS			

UK P&P: up to £24.99 = **£2.99**; £25.00 and over = **FREE**	
Elsewhere P&P: up to £10 = **£4.95**; £10.01 – £50 = **£6.95**; £50.01 – £99.99 = **£10**; £100 and over = **£30**	
Total Publications and P&P (please allow 14 days for delivery)	**A**	

Payment Details

☐ I enclose a cheque made payable to CWR for the amount of: **£**

☐ Please charge my credit/debit card.

Cardholder's Name (in BLOCK CAPITALS)

Card No. ☐☐☐☐ ☐☐☐☐ ☐☐☐☐ ☐☐☐☐

Expires End ☐☐ ☐☐   Security Code ☐☐☐

Continued overleaf >>

| One off Special Gift to Waverley Abbey Trust | ☐ Please send me an acknowledgement of my gift | **B** | |

GRAND TOTAL (Total of A & B)

Gift Aid (your home address required, see overleaf)

giftaid it

I am a UK taxpayer and want CWR to reclaim the tax on all my donations for the four years prior to this **and on** all donations I make from the date of this Gift Aid declaration until further notice.*

Taxpayer's Full Name (in BLOCK CAPITALS) _____

Signature _____ **Date** _____

*I am a UK taxpayer and understand that if I pay less Income Tax and/or Capital Gains Tax than the amount of Gift Aid claimed on all my donations in tha year it is my responsibility to pay any difference.

Your FREE Daily Bible Reading Notes Order

	Please Tick	FREE	£2 pcm	£5 pcm	£10 pcm	Other
Every Day with Jesus		☐	☐	☐	☐	☐ £ _____
Large Print *Every Day with Jesus*		☐	☐	☐	☐	☐ £ _____
Inspiring Women Every Day		☐	☐	☐	☐	☐ £ _____

All CWR Bible reading notes are also available in single issue **ebook** and **email subscription** format. Visit **waverleyabbeyresources.org** for further in

CWR — Instruction to your Bank or Building Society to pay by Direct Debit

DIREC Debi

Please fill in the form and send to: CWR, Waverley Abbey House, Waverley Lane, Farnham, Surrey GU9 8EP

Name and full postal address of your Bank or Building Society

To: The Manager   Bank/Building Society

Address

                              Postcode

Name(s) of Account Holder(s)

Branch Sort Code

Bank/Building Society Account Number

Originator's Identification Number

| 4 | 2 | 0 | 4 | 8 | 7 |

Reference

Instruction to your Bank or Building Society

Please pay CWR Direct Debits from the account detailed in this Instruc subject to the safeguards assured by the Direct Debit Guarantee. I understand that this Instruction may remain with CWR and, if so, detail will be passed electronically to my Bank/Building Society.

Signature(s)

Date

Banks and Building Societies may not accept Direct Debit Instructions for some types of account

For a subscription outside of the UK please visit www.waverleyabbeyresources.org where you will find a list of our national distributors.

How would you like to hear from us? We would love to keep you up to date on all aspects of the CWR ministry, including; new publications, events & courses as well as how you can support us.

If you **DO** want to hear from us on email, please tick here [ ]   If you **DO NOT** want us to contact you by post, please tick here

You can update your preferences at any time by contacting our customer services team on 01252 784 700. You can view our privacy policy online at waverleyabbeyresources.org